SCHOLASTIC

Perfect Poems

With Strategies for Building Fluency

Grades 1–2

NEW YORK • TORONTO • LONDON • AUCKLAND • SYDNEY
MEXICO CITY • NEW DELHI • HONG KONG • BUENOS AIRES

Teaching Resources

ACKNOWLEDGMENTS

Every effort has been made to contact copyright holders for permission to reproduce borrowed material. The publisher regrets any oversights that may have occurred and will be pleased to rectify them in subsequent reprints of the work.

The material on pages 4–13 has been adapted from BUILDING FLUENCY: LESSONS AND STRATEGIES FOR READING SUCCESS by Wiley Blevins (Scholastic, 2001). Adapted and reprinted by permission of the publisher.

"The Hare and the Tortoise" by Meish Goldish from ONCE UPON A TIME IN RHYME: 28 FOLK AND FAIRY TALE POEMS AND SONGS. Copyright © 1995 by Scholastic Inc. Used by permission of the publisher.

"Traffic Lights" by Vivian Gouled. Copyright © 1990 by Scholastic Inc. Used by permission of the publisher.

"I Play All Day" copyright © by Scholastic Inc. Used by permission of the publisher.

"What Do You Need?" by Helen O'Reilly from 70 WONDERFUL WORD FAMILY POEMS. Used by permission of Scholastic Inc.

"In the Box" copyright © by Scholastic Inc. Used by permission of the publisher.

"I Use My Brain" from THE COMPLETE BOOK OF RHYMES, SONGS, POEMS, FINGERPLAYS AND CHANTS by Jackie Silberg. Reprinted with permission from Gryphon House, P.O. Box 207, Beltsville, MD 20704-0207.

"Who Needs a Cook?" copyright © by Scholastic Inc. Used by permission of the publisher.

"I Had a Loose Tooth" by Lillie D. Chaffin. Copyright © 1990 by Scholastic Inc. Used by permission of the publisher.

"Baby Bear's Chicken Pox" from THE COMPLETE BOOK OF RHYMES, SONGS, POEMS, FINGERPLAYS AND CHANTS by Jackie Silberg. Reprinted with permission from Gryphon House, P.O. Box 207, Beltsville, MD 20704-0207.

"My Pets" by Elinor Chamas from THE GREAT BIG BOOK OF FUN PHONICS ACTIVITIES. Copyright © 1999 by Scholastic Inc. Used by permission of the publisher.

"Manners" copyright © 1997 by Helen H. Moore. Used by permission of the author.

"Rainy Day" copyright © 1999 by Mary Sullivan. Used by permission of the author.

"I See a Cat" by Cindy Chapman. Copyright © by Scholastic Inc. Used by permission of the publisher.

"It's Time" copyright © by Scholastic Inc. Used by permission of the publisher.

"Wishing for a Fish" copyright © by Scholastic Inc. Used by permission of the publisher.

"Red Hat" copyright © 1999 by Mary Sullivan. Used by permission of the author.

"Pumpkin Pie Time" copyright © 1998 by Dorothy Jean Sklar. Used by permission of the author.

"Roll, Roll, Roll the Snow" copyright © 1999 by Carol Pugliano-Martin. Used by permission of the author.

"Habitats" by Meish Goldish from ANIMAL POEMS FROM A TO Z. Copyright © 1994 by Scholastic Inc. Used by permission of the publisher.

"The Roundup" copyright © 1999 by Sheryl Ann Crawford and Nancy I. Sanders. Used by permission of the authors.

"Sing a Song of People" reprinted by permission of Lois Lenski Covey Foundation, c/o Arthur Abelman, Esq., Moses & Singer LLP.

Cover design by Maria Lilja
Interior illustrations by Maxi Chambliss, Kate Flanagan,
James Hale, Mark A. Hicks, Maggie Smith, and Bari Weissman
Interior design by Holly Grundon

ISBN: 0-439-43830-6

3 4 5 6 7 8 9 10   40   11 10 09 08 07 06 05 04

Contents

What Is Reading Fluency?

Fluency: A Definition

Listening to children read—whether it's a piece of their own writing or an excerpt from a favorite trade book can tell us a lot about their reading progress. An oral reading that is smooth, accurate, and that uses the correct intonation and phrasing reflects a reader who understands the text and has mastered basic decoding skills. An oral reading that is slow, labored, and lacking in expression is characteristic of a child who lacks reading proficiency or is reading a text beyond his or her reading level. Therefore, a child's reading fluency is one important measure of a child's reading progress.

According to *A Dictionary of Reading and Related Terms* (Harris and Hodges, 1981), fluency is "the ability to read smoothly, easily, and readily with freedom from word-recognition problems." Fluency is necessary for good comprehension and enjoyable reading (Nathan and Stanovich, 1991). A lack of fluency is characterized by a slow, halting pace; frequent mistakes; poor phrasing; and inadequate intonation (Samuels, 1979)—all the result of weak word-recognition skills.

Fluent reading is a major goal of reading instruction because decoding print accurately and effortlessly enables students to read for meaning. According to Chall's Stages of Reading Development, fluency begins around grades 2 to 3 for many students. During this fluency stage, the reader becomes "unglued" from the print; that is, students can recognize many words quickly and accurately by sight and are skilled at sounding out those they don't recognize. The decoding work done in grades 1 and 2 lays the foundation for a student's fluency. Therefore, students need many reading opportunities and ample explicit phonics instruction to become proficient decoders. Basically, a fluent reader can:

1. **read at a rapid rate (pace—the speed at which oral or silent reading occurs).**

2. **automatically recognize words (smoothness/accuracy— efficient decoding skills).**

3. **phrase correctly (prosody—the ability to read a text orally using appropriate pitch, stress, and phrasing).**

Nonfluent readers read slowly and spend so much time trying to identify unfamiliar words that they have trouble comprehending what they're reading.

Automaticity theory, developed by LaBerge and Samuels (1974) helps explain how reading fluency develops. Automaticity refers to knowing how to do something so well you don't have to think about it. As tasks become easier, they require less attention and practice. Think of a child learning to play basketball. As initial attention is focused on how to dribble the ball, it's difficult for the child to think about guarding the ball from opponents, shooting a basket, or even running quickly down the court. However, over time, lots of practice makes dribbling almost second nature. The player is ready to concentrate on higher-level aspects of the game.

For reading, automaticity refers to the ability to accurately and quickly recognize many words as whole units. The advantage of recognizing a word as a whole unit is that words have meaning, and less memory is required for a meaningful word than for a meaningless letter. The average child needs between 4 and 14 exposures to a new word to recognize it automatically. However, children with reading difficulties need 40 or more exposures to a new word. Therefore, it's critical that students get a great deal of practice reading texts at their independent reading level to develop automaticity (Beck & Juel, 1995; Samuels, Schermer & Reinking, 1992).

To commit words to memory, children need to decode many words sound by sound, and then progress to recognizing the larger word chunks. Then, instead of focusing on sounding out words sound by sound, the reader can read whole words, thereby focusing attention on decoding and comprehension simultaneously. In fact, the hallmark of fluent reading is the ability to decode and comprehend at the same time.

Although research has shown that fluency is a critical factor in reading development, many teachers and publishers have failed to recognize its importance to overall reading proficiency. Few teachers teach fluency directly, and elementary reading textbooks give fluency instruction short shrift. Consequently, Allington (1983) has called fluency the "neglected goal" of reading instruction.

There are many reasons why children fail to read fluently. They include the following (Allington, 1983; Blevins, 2002):

Lack of foundational skills

Some children have not mastered basic decoding skills or sight word recognition of the most frequent words in text. Therefore, when they are confronted with more complex text containing longer sentences and more multisyllabic words, their reading breaks down.

Lack of practice time

Good readers generally spend more time reading during instructional time and therefore become better readers. Good readers also engage in more silent reading. This additional practice stimulates their reading growth. Poor readers spend less time actually reading.

Frustration

Good readers are exposed to more text at their independent reading level, whereas poor readers frequently encounter text at their frustration level. Consequently poor readers tend to give up because they make so many errors.

Lack of exposure

Some children have never been exposed to fluent reading models. These children come from homes in which there are few books and little or no reading.

Missing the "why" of reading

Good readers tend to view reading as making meaning from text, whereas poor readers tend to view reading as trying to read words accurately.

The good-reader syndrome

In school, good readers are more likely to get positive feedback and more likely to be encouraged to read with expression and make meaning from text. Poor readers receive less positive feedback and the focus of their instruction is often solely on figuring out words or attending to word parts.

How to Develop Fluency

Although few reading-textbook teacher manuals contain instruction on building fluency, there are in fact many things you can do to develop your students' fluency. Rasinski (1989) has identified six key ways to build fluency.

1. Model fluent reading

Students need many opportunities to hear texts read. This can include daily teacher read alouds, books on tape, poems, and texts read by peers during sharing time. It's particularly critical for poorer readers who've been placed in a low reading group to hear text read correctly because they are likely to repeatedly hear the efforts of other poor readers in their group. They need proficient, fluent models; that is, they need to have a model voice in their heads to refer to as they monitor their own reading. While you read aloud to students, periodically highlight aspects of fluent reading. For example, point out how you read dialogue the way you think the character might have said it or how you speed up your reading when the text becomes more intense and exciting. Talk about fluency—how to achieve it, and why it's important. Constantly remind students that with practice they can become fluent readers. An important benefit of daily read alouds is that they expose students to a wider range of vocabulary.

2. Provide direct instruction and feedback

Direct instruction and feedback in fluency includes, but isn't limited to, independent reading practice, fluent reading modeling, and monitoring students' reading rates. Here are some ways to include lots of this needed instruction in your classroom.

- ✸ Explicitly teach students sound-spelling correspondences they struggle with, high-utility decoding and syllabication strategies, and a large core of sight words.

- ✸ Occasionally time students' reading. Have students create charts to monitor their own progress. Encourage them to set new reading-rate goals.

- ✸ Find alternatives to round-robin reading. Round-robin reading is one of the most harmful techniques for developing fluency. During round-robin reading, students read aloud only a small portion of the text. Although they are supposed to be following along with the other readers, often they don't. It is absolutely essential that students read a lot every day. When they're reading a new story or poem, it is important that they read the entire text—often more than once. One way to avoid round-robin reading is to have students read the text silently a few pages at a time and then ask them questions or have them comment on strategies they used. Other appropriate techniques include partner reading, reading softly to themselves while you circulate and "listen in," and popcorn reading, in which students are called on frequently and randomly (often in the middle of a paragraph or stanza) to read aloud. If you use any technique in which students have not read the entire text during their reading group, be sure that they read it in its entirety before or after the reading group.

❀ Teach appropriate phrasing and intonation. Guided oral reading practice and the study of punctuation and grammar can help. For teaching phrasing, see phrase-cued text practice on page 11. For teaching intonation and punctuation, use some or all of the following. Have students:

◆ recite the alphabet as a conversation.
ABCD? EFG! HI? JKL. MN? OPQ. RST! UVWX. YZ!

◆ recite the same sentence using different punctuation.
Cows moo. Cows moo? Cows moo!

◆ practice placing the stress on different words in the same sentence.
I am happy. I <u>am</u> happy. I am <u>happy</u>.

◆ practice reading sentences as if talking to a friend.

Studying grammar fosters fluency because grammar alerts the reader to natural phrases in a sentence. For example, being able to identify the subject and the predicate of a sentence is one step in understanding phrase boundaries in text. Also, understanding the role of prepositions and conjunctions adds additional clues to phrase boundaries. Try providing students with short passages color-coded according to subject and predicate to assist them in practice reading.

❀ Conduct 2-minute drills to underline or locate a target word, syllable, or spelling pattern in an array or short passage (Moats, 1998). This will help students rapidly recognize spelling patterns that are common to many words. And it's a lot of fun.

3. Provide reader support (choral reading and reading-while-listening)

Readers need to practice reading both orally and silently. Research has shown that oral reading is very important for the developing reader, especially younger children. It appears that young children need to hear themselves read, and they benefit from adult feedback. As well as improving reading, this feedback shows students how highly we adults value the skill of reading. There are several ways to support students' oral reading without evoking the fear and humiliation struggling readers often feel when called on to read aloud. Here are the most popular techniques (always use text at the student's instructional level that models natural language patterns).

❀ Reading simultaneously with a partner or small group. With this technique, students can "float" in and out as appropriate without feeling singled out. For best results, have students practice reading the selection independently before reading it with the partner or group.

❀ Echo reading. As you read a phrase or sentence in the text, the student repeats it. This continues throughout the text. You can also use a tape recording of the text with pauses for the child to echo the reading.

❀ Choral reading. Reading together as a group is great for poetry and selections with a distinct pattern. Students are challenged to read at the same pace and with the same phrasing and intonation as the rest of the group.

❀ Paired repeated readings (Koskinen and Blum, 1986). A student reads a short text three times to a partner and gets feedback. Then the partners switch roles. To avoid frustration, it works best to pair above-level readers with on-level readers and on-level readers with below-level readers.

❀ Books and poems on tape. Select and place appropriate books and poems on tape in a classroom Listening Center. Have students follow along as the text is read, reading with the narrator where possible.

4. Repeated readings of one text

Repeated reading, a popular technique developed by Samuels (1979), has long been recognized as an excellent way to help students achieve fluency. It has been shown to increase reading rate and accuracy and to transfer to new texts. As a child reads a passage at his or her instructional level, the teacher times the reading. The teacher then gives feedback on word-recognition errors and the number of words per minute the child read accurately, and records this data on a graph. (To use poetry for repeated readings in grades 1–2, the poem should contain about 100 words.) The child then practices reading the same selection independently or with a partner. The process is repeated and the child's progress plotted on the graph until the child masters the text. This charting is effective because (1) students become focused on their own mastery of the task and competing with their own past performance, and (2) students have concrete evidence that they are making progress. In addition, repeating the words many times helps students build a large sight-word vocabulary.

Students who resist rereading selections need incentives. Besides simply telling the student that rereading is a part of the important practice one does to become a better reader, you might motivate her by having her:

◆ read to a friend, family member, or pet,

◆ read to a student in a lower grade,

◆ read into a tape player to record the session,

◆ set a reading-rate goal for a given piece of text and try to exceed that goal in successive readings.

Repeated-Reading Chart

Name Maria Gonzales
Beginning Date Febrary 10
Ending Date Febrary 14
Book Roll, Roll, Roll The Snow
Number of Words Correctly Read in One Minute _____

Number of Trials

5. Cueing phrase boundaries in text

One of the characteristics of proficient (fluent) readers is the ability to group words together in meaningful units—syntactically appropriate phrases. "Proficient reading is characterized not only by fast and accurate word recognition, but also by readers' word chunking or phrasing behavior while reading connected discourse." (Rasinski, 1989) Students who are having trouble with comprehension may not be putting words together in meaningful phrases or chunks as they read. Their oral reading is characterized by a choppy, word-by-word delivery that impedes comprehension. These students need instruction in phrasing written text into appropriate segments.

One way to help students learn to recognize and use natural English phrase boundaries—and thus improve their phrasing, fluency, and comprehension—is phrase-cued text practice. Phrase-cued text is a short passage marked by a slash (or some other visual) at the end of each phrase break. The longer pause at the end of the sentence is marked by a double slash (//). The teacher models good oral reading, and students practice with the marked text. Later, students apply their skills to the same text, unmarked. Have students practice the skill orally for 10 minutes daily.

Here's an example:

In the summer/I like/to swim/at the beach.//

Although it's very hot/I like the idea/

of being in the cool water

all day.// Summer truly is/

my favorite time/of the year.//

6. Providing students with easy reading materials

Students need an enormous amount of individualized reading practice in decodable materials that are not too difficult (Beck & Juel, 1995; Samuels, Schermer & Reinking, 1992). Aim for at least 30 minutes of independent reading every day. Some should occur in school, and some can occur at home. Fluency develops through a great deal of practice reading texts in which students can use sound-spelling strategies (as opposed to contextual strategies) to figure out a majority of the unfamiliar words. In the early grades, there must be a match between instruction in phonics and reading practice—hence the need for practice stories and poems that are decodable (Blevins, 2002). This match encourages students to adopt sound-spelling strategies and at the same time, through extensive practice reading text after text after text, leads to fluent reading. It is critical that practice reading materials be at a child's independent or instructional reading level, *not* at the child's frustration level. In other words, the student's reading accuracy (the proportion of words read correctly) should be above 90 percent. During individualized practice, students may be reading at different levels. They read aloud "quietly" to themselves as the teacher walks around listening to each child for a minute or so while still monitoring the group as a whole. Students need time to figure out unfamiliar words through phonics patterns. Expecting students to read fluently when they are not fluent only encourages guessing and memorization.

Using Poetry to Build Fluency

Poetry lends itself beautifully to fluency instruction and practice. The length and natural rhythms of most poems give them a musical quality that's enjoyable to listen to and perform. Poetry often contains a wide range of punctuation and phrasing, two key aspects of fluency. In addition, poems are fun ways to practice one's decoding skills.

The poems in this collection are divided into four categories:

1. Poems for Partners and Small Groups

These poems are ideal for students to read together. Some contain multiple parts perfect for Reader's Theater; others have repetitive stanzas that are fun for choral reading. Working together gives students an opportunity to provide peers with constructive feedback, thereby verbalizing their understanding of fluent reading.

2. Poems to Build Intonation and Phrasing

These poems focus on varying the pace and expression of oral readings. The variety of sentence types and phrase boundaries helps students to pay attention to these important aspects of reading. In addition, the chunking of text into meaningful units, line by line, is one way to introduce or reinforce aspects of grammar useful in reading fluently (subject, predicate, prepositional phrases).

3. Poems to Build Recognition of Phonics Patterns and Sight Words

These poems focus on one or two key phonics patterns common to early reading materials. The repetition of the patterns helps students to easily recognize these larger word chunks so useful in decoding longer words.

4. Poems for Repeated Readings

These poems are more complex and comprehensive. They require students to pull together all aspects of fluent reading and encourage students to practice enough so that a formal, dramatic reading is the ultimate result.

Instructional Routine

Use the following routine for introducing each poem.

STEP 1: Distribute copies of the poem or write the poem on chart paper. As an alternative, make a transparency of the poem and show it on the overhead projector.

STEP 2: Read aloud the poem. Highlight one or two aspects of fluency, such as intonation or phrasing. Discuss these aspects of fluency and model them using selected sentences or phrases from the poem.

STEP 3: Do an echo reading of the poem. Read aloud each stanza and have students repeat using the same pace, accuracy, and expression.

STEP 4: Assign the poem to partners, small groups, or individuals based on the goal of each poem. For example, poems designed for repeated readings should be assigned to individuals, whereas poems for choral readings should be assigned to small groups.

STEP 5: Provide time throughout the week for students to practice reading aloud their poems. Circulate and listen in. Provide feedback on key aspects of fluent reading. Then, allow students to share their readings at the end of the week.

Above all, have fun with the poems in this book. Poems are like language amusement parks; they represent the works of those playing with language in rhythmic and creative ways. Sharing the joys of written language with students is a wonderful and valuable gift.

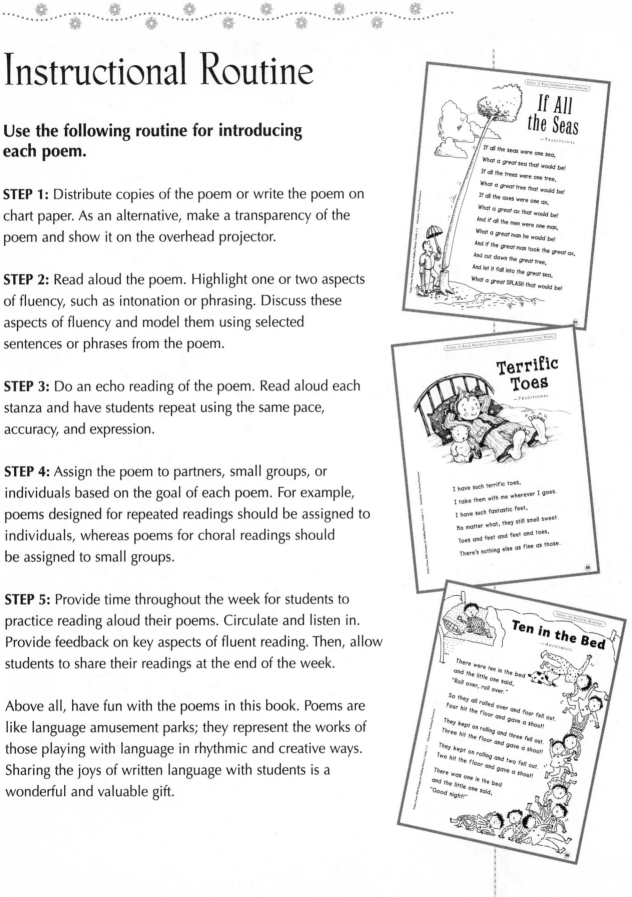

Did You Feed My Cow?

—Traditional

Did you feed my cow?

    Yes, Ma'am!

Will you tell me how?

    Yes, Ma'am!

Oh, what did you give her?

    Corn and hay.

Oh, what did you give her?

    Corn and hay.

Did you milk her good?

    Yes, Ma'am!

Did you do like you should?

    Yes, Ma'am!

Oh, how did you milk her?

    Swish! Swish! Swish!

Oh, how did you milk her?

    Swish! Swish! Swish!

Perfect Poems With Strategies for Building Fluency: Grades 1–2 Scholastic Teaching Resources

Ten Tall Firefighters

—TRADITIONAL

Ten tall firefighters
sleeping in a row.
"Ding" goes the bell
and down the pole they go.
They jump into their fire trucks
with no delay.
The sirens warn everyone
to get out of the way.

With water from the big hoses
they put the fire out.
"Hurrah, hurrah, brave firefighters!"
all the people shout.
Then back to the station
Go ten tired firefighters
To sleep until the bell
Wakes them up again.

15

Walking, Walking

—TRADITIONAL

Walking, walking,

walking, walking.

Hop, hop, hop,

hop, hop, hop.

Running, running, running,

running, running, running.

Now let's stop,

now let's stop.

Perfect Poems With Strategies for Building Fluency: Grades 1–2   Scholastic Teaching Resources

The Hare
and the Tortoise

BY MEISH GOLDISH

Teacher: Did you hear about the race
between Tortoise and Hare?

Students: *Go, go, go! Go, go, go!*

Teacher: No one thought it would be fair.

Students: *No, no, no! No, no, no!*

Teacher: Hare was fast with legs so strong.

Students: *Go, go, go! Go, go, go!*

Teacher: Tortoise only crept along.

Students: *Slow, slow, slow! Slow, slow, slow!*

Continued

Teacher: Round the lake they went to race,

Students: *Go, go, go! Go, go, go!*

Teacher: Each one at a different pace.

Students: *Oh, oh, oh! Oh, oh, oh!*

Teacher: Hare was so sure he was best,

Students: *Go, go, go! Go, go, go!*

Teacher: He ran ahead, then stopped to rest.

Students: *Whoa, whoa, whoa! Whoa, whoa, whoa!*

Teacher: Meanwhile Tortoise slowly crept,

Students: *Slow, slow, slow! Slow, slow, slow!*

Teacher: Passing Hare who soundly slept.

Students: *Oh, oh, oh! Oh, oh, oh!*

Teacher: Guess which runner took first place?

Students: *Go, go, go! Go, go, go!*

Teacher: Slow and steady wins the race.

Students: *Ho, ho, ho! Ho, ho, ho!*

Traffic Lights

BY VIVIAN GOULED

Red light, red light,
What do you say?
I say, "Stop,
And stop right away!"

Yellow light, yellow light,
What do you mean?
I mean "Wait—
Till the light turns green!"

Green light, green light,
What do you say?
I say, "Cross!
First look each way!"

Thank you, thank you,
Red, yellow, green;
Now I know
What traffic lights mean!

I Play All Day

The rain can fall.

The sun can go away.

But I don't stop.

I play all day.

My feet can get wet.

The day can get gray.

But I don't stop.

I play all day.

Some kids go inside.

Some kids may not stay.

But I don't stop.

I play all day!

Perfect Poems With Strategies for Building Fluency: Grades 1–2   Scholastic Teaching Resources

Zip, Zoom

—TRADITIONAL

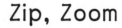

Zip, Zoom

Zip, Zoom

Zip, Zoom

The buzzing bee

Flew through my room.

Zip, Zee

Zip, Zee

Zip, Zee

It flew out the window

And up the tree.

Zip, Zoom, Zee!

Miss Polly Had a Dolly

—TRADITIONAL

Miss Polly had a dolly

Who was sick, sick, sick,

So she called for the doctor

To be quick, quick, quick;

The doctor came

With his bag and his hat,

And he knocked at the door

With a rat-a-tat-tat.

He looked at the dolly

And he shook his head,

And he said, "Miss Polly,

Put her straight to bed."

He wrote out a paper

For a pill, pill, pill.

"That'll make her better,

Yes it will, will, will!"

Perfect Poems With Strategies for Building Fluency: Grades 1–2   Scholastic Teaching Resources

22

What Do You Need?

BY HELEN O'REILLY

To build a house

You need a block.

To tell the time

You need a clock.

To open the door

You need to knock.

To sail a ship

You need a dock.

And to cover your foot,

You need a sock.

Block, clock,

Tick tock,

Knock, dock

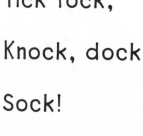

Sock!

In the Box

In the box I had

ten cats,

ten dogs,

ten hats,

and

ten logs,

ten wigs,

ten nets,

ten pigs,

and

ten jets.

In the box,

I had a lot!

Perfect Poems With Strategies for Building Fluency: Grades 1–2 Scholastic Teaching Resources

I Use My Brain

BY JACKIE SILBERG

I use my brain to think, think, think.

I use my nose to smell.

I use my eyes to blink, blink, blink.

I use my throat to yell.

I use my mouth to giggle, giggle, giggle.

I use my hips to bump.

I use my toes to wiggle, wiggle, wiggle,

And I use my legs to jump.

Five Little Monkeys

—TRADITIONAL

Five little monkeys
Sitting in a tree
Teasing Mr. Crocodile—
"You can't catch me.
You can't catch me."
Along comes Mr. Crocodile
As quiet as can be—
SNAP!

Four little monkeys
Sitting in a tree
Teasing Mr. Crocodile—
"You can't catch me.
You can't catch me."
Along comes Mr. Crocodile
As quiet as can be—
SNAP!

Continued

Perfect Poems With Strategies for Building Fluency: Grades 1–2   Scholastic Teaching Resources

Three little monkeys
Sitting in a tree
Teasing Mr. Crocodile—
"You can't catch me.
You can't catch me."
Along comes Mr. Crocodile
As quiet as can be—
SNAP!

Two little monkeys
Sitting in a tree
Teasing Mr. Crocodile—
"You can't catch me.
You can't catch me."
Along comes Mr. Crocodile
As quiet as can be—
SNAP!

Continued

One little monkey
Sitting in a tree
Teasing Mr. Crocodile—
"You can't catch me.
You can't catch me."
Along comes Mr. Crocodile
As quiet as can be—
SNAP!

Away swims Mr. Crocodile
As full as can be!

Perfect Poems With Strategies for Building Fluency: Grades 1–2   Scholastic Teaching Resources

Who Needs a Cook?

The clock says noon.

It's time for lunch.

We have forks and spoons,

We're all set to munch.

Now where's the cook?

Well, who needs her?

We'll look in the book

And mix and stir.

What a mess of goop!

Get the dust pan and the broom!

We'll sweep and scoop,

And clean it up soon.

Oops!

What the Animals Say

—Traditional

Little pup, little pup,
What do you say?
"Woof, woof, woof!
Let's go and play."

Kittycat, kittycat,
How about you?
"Meow, meow, meow!
And I purr, too."

Pretty bird, pretty bird,
Have you a song?
"Tweet, tweet, tweet!
The whole day long."

Continued

Jersey cow, Jersey cow,
What do you do?
"Moo, moo, moo!
And give milk, too."

Little lamb, little lamb,
What do you say?
"Baa, baa, baa!
Can Mary play?"

Spring Is Coming

—TRADITIONAL

Spring is coming, spring is coming!

How do you think I know?

I see a flower blooming,

I know it must be so.

Spring is coming, spring is coming!

How do you think I know?

I see a blossom on the tree,

I know it must be so.

Perfect Poems With Strategies for Building Fluency: Grades 1–2   Scholastic Teaching Resources

I Had a Loose Tooth

BY LILLIE D. CHAFFIN

I had a loose tooth,

A wiggly, jiggly loose tooth.

I had a loose tooth,

A-hanging by a thread.

I pulled my loose tooth,

My wiggly, jiggly loose tooth.

Put it 'neath my pillow,

And then I went to bed.

The fairy took my loose tooth,

My wiggly, jiggly loose tooth.

And now I have a quarter,

And a hole in my head.

Baby Bear's
Chicken Pox

BY JACKIE SILBERG

"Waa, waa, waa," cried baby bear.

"I've got chicken pox in my hair.

On my nose and everywhere.

Waa, waa, waa," cried baby bear.

"Oh poor baby," Mommy said.

"Come to me and rest your head.

Soon you will be out of bed.

Oh poor baby," Mommy said.

Perfect Poems With Strategies for Building Fluency: Grades 1–2 Scholastic Teaching Resources

My Pets

BY ELINOR CHAMAS

My duck ate my cake,

My dog ate my ham,

My cat stole my milk,

And my bee is on my jam.

My pig has my pancake,

My mice got my cheese,

Tell me, why, oh why,

Did I choose pets like these?

Perfect Poems With Strategies for Building Fluency: Grades 1–2   Scholastic Teaching Resources

Once I Saw a Little Bird

—TRADITIONAL

Once I saw a little bird

Come hop, hop, hop.

And I cried, "Little bird,

Will you stop, stop, stop?"

I was going to the window

To say, "How do you do?"

When he shook his little tail,

And away he flew.

Perfect Poems With Strategies for Building Fluency: Grades 1–2   Scholastic Teaching Resources

If All the Seas

—TRADITIONAL

If all the seas were one sea,

What a *great* sea that would be!

If all the trees were one tree,

What a *great* tree that would be!

If all the axes were one ax,

What a *great* ax that would be!

And if all the men were one man,

What a *great* man he would be!

And if the *great* man took the *great* ax,

And cut down the *great* tree,

And let it fall into the *great* sea,

What a *great* SPLASH that would be!

Manners

BY HELEN H. MOORE

We say "Thank you."

We say, "Please,"

And "Excuse me"

When we sneeze.

That's the way

We do what's right.

We have manners.

We're polite.

Five Little Owls

—ANONYMOUS

Five little owls in an old elm tree,

Fluffy and puffy as owls could be.

Blinking and winking with big round eyes

At the big round moon that hung in the skies.

As I passed I could hear one say,

"There will be mouse for supper,

There will, today!"

Then all of them hooted,

"Tu-whit, tu-whoo,

Yes, mouse for supper,

Hoo, hoo, hoo, hoo!"

Rainy Day

BY MARY SULLIVAN

Plip! Plop!

Raindrop.

I'll stay inside today.

Plip! Plop!

Raindrop.

I'll call a friend to play.

Plip! Plop!

Raindrop.

I know my friend will say:

"Plip! Plop!

Raindrop.

We'll have fun today!"

Perfect Poems With Strategies for Building Fluency: Grades 1–2 Scholastic Teaching Resources

Mix a Pancake

BY CHRISTINA G. ROSSETTI

Mix a pancake,

Stir a pancake,

    Pop it in the pan;

Fry the pancake,

Toss the pancake,

    Catch it if you can.

I See a Cat

BY CINDY CHAPMAN

I see a cat.

I see a big cat.

I see a big, fat cat.

I see a big, fat cat on a mat.

I see a big, fat cat on my lap!

I see a rat.

I see a big rat.

I see a big, fat rat.

I see a big, fat rat on a mat.

I will NOT see a big, fat rat on MY LAP!

Perfect Poems With Strategies for Building Fluency: Grades 1–2   Scholastic Teaching Resources

The Alphabet
Forward and Backwards

—TRADITIONAL

A - B - C - D - E - F - G,

H - I - J - K - L - M - N - O - P,

Q - R - S,

T - U - V,

W - X,

Y and Z.

Now I know my ABCs.

Next time sing them backwards with me.

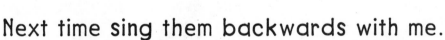

Continued

Z - Y - X - W - V - U - T

S - R - Q - P - O - N - M - L - K

J - I - H,

G - F - E,

D - C,

B and A

Now I've said my ZYXs.

Bet that's not what you expected!

Perfect Poems With Strategies for Building Fluency: Grades 1–2   Scholastic Teaching Resources

Good Morning, Mrs. Hen —TRADITIONAL

Good morning, Mrs. Hen.

How many chickens have you got?

Madam, I've got ten;

Four of them yellow,

Four of them brown,

And two of them are speckled red,

The nicest in the town.

My Big Balloon

—TRADITIONAL

I can make a big balloon.

Watch me while I blow.

Small at first, then bigger.

Watch it grow and grow.

Do you think it's big enough?

Maybe I should stop.

For if I blow much longer,

My balloon will surely POP!

Perfect Poems With Strategies for Building Fluency: Grades 1–2   Scholastic Teaching Resources

It's Time

The bugs ride a bike.

The bugs bake a cake.

The bugs take a hike.

They run to the lake.

The bugs see the time.

The bugs have a date.

The bugs run home to dine.

They hate to be late.

Perfect Poems With Strategies for Building Fluency: Grades 1–2   Scholastic Teaching Resources

August Heat

—TRADITIONAL

In August, when the days are hot,

I like to find a shady spot

And hardly move a single bit.

And sit.

And sit.

And sit.

And sit!

Perfect Poems With Strategies for Building Fluency: Grades 1–2   Scholastic Teaching Resources

Rags

—Traditional

I have a dog and his name is Rags.

He eats so much that his tummy sags.

His ears flip-flop,

And his tail wig-wags,

And when he walks,

He goes zig-zag.

Thank You

—TRADITIONAL

My hands say thank you

With a clap, clap, clap.

My feet say thank you

With a tap, tap, tap.

Clap, clap, clap.

Tap, tap, tap.

I turn around,

Touch the ground,

And with a bow,

I say . . . "Thank you, now."

Perfect Poems With Strategies for Building Fluency: Grades 1–2   Scholastic Teaching Resources

Wishing for a Fish

I am wishing for a fish.

I will not quit.

I am wishing for a fish.

I sit and sit.

I am wishing for a fish.

I will not rush.

I am wishing for a fish.

Shh . . . hush, hush, hush.

Did I get one?

Red Hat

BY MARY SULLIVAN

Red hat, red hair,

Red mat, red chair.

Red bug, red spot,

Red rug, red dots.

Red face, red feather,

Red lace, red leather.

Red nose, red mitt,

Red rose, let's quit!

Perfect Poems With Strategies for Building Fluency: Grades 1–2   Scholastic Teaching Resources

Terrific Toes

—TRADITIONAL

I have such terrific toes,

I take them with me wherever I goes.

I have such fantastic feet,

No matter what, they still smell sweet.

Toes and feet and feet and toes,

There's nothing else as fine as those.

From
Over in the Meadow

BY OLIVE A. WADSWORTH

Over in the meadow
in the sand in the sun,
lived an old mother toadie
and her little toadie one.
"Hop," said the mother.
"I hop," said the one.
So they hopped and were glad
in the sand in the sun.

Over in the meadow
where the stream runs blue,
lived an old mother fish
and her little fishes two.
"Swim!" said the mother,
"We swim!" said the two.
So they swam and they leaped
where the stream runs blue.

Continued

Perfect Poems With Strategies for Building Fluency: Grades 1–2 Scholastic Teaching Resources

Over in the meadow
in the nest in the tree,
lived an old mother birdy
and her little birdies three.
"Sing," said the mother.
"We sing," said the three.
So they sang and were glad
in the nest in the tree.

Pumpkin Pie Time

BY DOROTHY JEAN SKLAR

Thanksgiving's coming.

It's time to bake pies.

Apple and pumpkin

Are sure to delight!

Slice up the apples

(sneak a tiny bite!).

Mash up the pumpkin

(one that's plump and ripe).

Add a bit of sugar.

Sprinkle in some spice.

Roll out the pie crust.

Make it thin and light.

Bake the pies in the oven

'til they're browned just right.

Set them on the table.

Oh, they smell so nice!

Now, come one, come all,

And bring your appetite!

Perfect Poems With Strategies for Building Fluency: Grades 1–2   Scholastic Teaching Resources

Peanut Butter and Jelly

—ANONYMOUS

First you take the dough

and knead it, knead it.

Peanut butter, peanut butter, jelly, jelly.

Pop it in the oven

and bake it, bake it.

Peanut butter, peanut butter, jelly, jelly.

Then you take a knife

and slice it, slice it.

Peanut butter, peanut butter, jelly, jelly.

Then you take the peanuts

and crack them, crack them.

Peanut butter, peanut butter, jelly, jelly.

Continued

Put them on the floor

and mash them, mash them.

Peanut butter, peanut butter, jelly, jelly.

Then you take a knife

and spread it, spread it.

Peanut butter, peanut butter, jelly, jelly.

Next you take some grapes

and squash them, squash them.

Peanut butter, peanut butter, jelly, jelly.

Glop it on the bread

and smear it, smear it.

Peanut butter, peanut butter, jelly, jelly.

Then you take the sandwich

and eat it, eat it.

Peanut butter, peanut butter, jelly, jelly.

Perfect Poems With Strategies for Building Fluency: Grades 1–2   Scholastic Teaching Resources

Ten in the Bed

—ANONYMOUS

There were ten in the bed
and the little one said,
"Roll over, roll over."

So they all rolled over and four fell out.
Four hit the floor and gave a shout!

They kept on rolling and three fell out.
Three hit the floor and gave a shout!

They kept on rolling and two fell out.
Two hit the floor and gave a shout!

There was one in the bed
and the little one said,
"Good night!"

Roll, Roll, Roll the Snow!

BY CAROL PUGLIANO-MARTIN

Roll, roll, roll the snow,

Make a big snowball.

Make two more and stack them up

So that they won't fall.

Roll, roll, roll the snow,

Each arm will be a stick.

One on the left, one on the right,

That will do the trick!

Continued

Perfect Poems With Strategies for Building Fluency: Grades 1–2   Scholastic Teaching Resources

Roll, roll, roll the snow,
Add some button eyes.
Now he's looking right at me
What a nice surprise!

Roll, roll, roll the snow,
A carrot for the nose.
Make a mouth out of some coal.
Now we need some clothes!

Roll, roll, roll the snow,
Add a scarf and hat.
We have made a great snowman,
And that's the end of that!

Habitats

BY MEISH GOLDISH

Home, sweet home!

Home, sweet animal home!

Birds like to rest

In a twiggy nest.

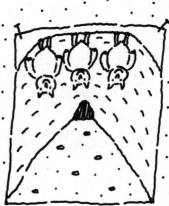

A big brown bear

Prefers a lair.

Bats love to rave

About their cave!

Monkeys swing free

High in a tree!

The tiny frog

Lives on a log.

Continued

Perfect Poems With Strategies for Building Fluency: Grades 1–2   Scholastic Teaching Resources

Chipmunks are found

In a hole in the ground.

Home in a thicket?

A lion would pick it!

The crab lives well

In an empty shell.

A hive will please

A family of bees.

Is *your* home the home

For dogs or cats?

Animals have

many habitats!

Tiny Tim

—TRADITIONAL

I had a little turtle,

His name was Tiny Tim.

I put him in the bathtub,

To see if he could swim.

He drank up all the water,

He ate up all the soap.

Tiny Tim was choking

On the bubbles in his throat!

In came the doctor,

In came the nurse,

In came the lady

With the alligator purse.

Continued

They pumped out all the water,

They pumped out all the soap,

They popped the airy bubbles

As they floated from his throat.

Out went the doctor,

Out went the nurse,

Out went the lady

With the alligator purse!

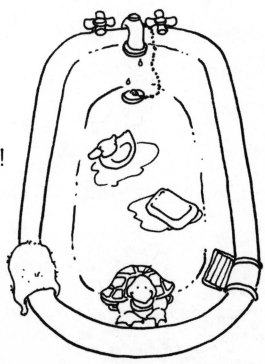

I Went Downtown

—ANONYMOUS

I went downtown
To see Mrs. Brown.

She gave me a nickel
To buy a pickle.

The pickle was sour,
She gave me a flower.

The flower was dead,
She gave me a thread.

The thread was thin,
She gave me a pin.

The pin was sharp,
She gave me a harp.

She gave me a harp
And the harp began to sing—
Minnie and a minnie
And a ha ha ha!

The Roundup

BY SHERYL ANN CRAWFORD AND NANCY I. SANDERS

Yippee-yi-yi-yea!

Here's our big chance:

We'll round up twelve cows and

Bring them back to the ranch!

Jingle your spurs!

Hold on to your chaps.

We're rounding up cattle and

Bringing them back!

We found all twelve.

Now isn't that great!

I'll round up these four cows.

You round up those eight.

Jingle your spurs!

Hold on to your chaps.

We're rounding up cattle and

Bringing them back!

Continued

Let's cross this river.

Listen to them moo!

One dozen cattle

In six groups of two.

They're kicking up trail dust.

It's getting hard to see!

Divide those cattle

Into four groups of three.

All twelve cattle

Thunder through the gate.

One cow at a time

In a line nice and straight.

Jingle your spurs!

Hold on to your chaps.

We rounded up twelve cows

And brought them all back.

The roundup is done.

It's been quite a day!

Let's kick off our boots!

Yippee-yi-yi-yea!

Perfect Poems With Strategies for Building Fluency: Grades 1–2   Scholastic Teaching Resources

Butter

BY JANET SMALLEY

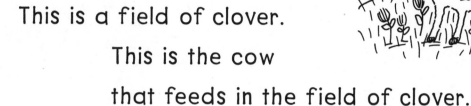

This is a field of clover.

   This is the cow

   that feeds in the field of clover.

This is the milk

that comes from the cow

that feeds in the field of clover.

   This is the cream

   that comes on the milk

   that comes from the cow

   that feeds in the field of clover.

Continued

This is the churn

that churns the cream

that comes on the milk

that comes from the cow

that feeds in the field of clover.

This is the butter

that comes from the churn

that churns the cream

that comes on the milk

that comes from the cow

that feeds in the field of clover.

These are the hot cakes

that melt the butter

that comes from the churn

that churns the cream

that comes on the milk

that comes from the cow

that feeds in the field of clover.

Perfect Poems With Strategies for Building Fluency: Grades 1–2   Scholastic Teaching Resources

Sing a Song of People

BY LOIS LENSKI

Sing a song of people
　　Walking fast or slow;
People in the city,
　　Up and down they go.

　　People on the sidewalk,
　　People on the bus;
　　People passing, passing,
In back and front of us.
People on the subway
Underneath the ground;
People riding taxis
Round and round and round.

　　People with their hats on,
　　Going in the doors;
　　People with umbrellas
　　When it rains and pours.

Continued

People in tall buildings
And in stores below;
Riding elevators
Up and down they go.

People walking singly,
People in a crowd;
People saying nothing,
People talking loud.
People laughing, smiling,
Grumpy people, too;
People who just hurry
And never look at you!

Sing a song of people
    Who like to come and go;
Sing of city people
    You see but never know!

Perfect Poems With Strategies for Building Fluency: Grades 1–2   Scholastic Teaching Resources